Grade 3 Piano
Sight Reading Intensive Exercise

(Based on ABRSM Grade 3
Piano Sight Reading Syllabus)

Regina Pratley

ISBN: 1546364706
ISBN-13: 978-1546364702

DEDICATION

Dedicated to all the students that are going to take the ABRSM grade 3 piano exam.
Wishing you all the best in the exam! ☺

CONTENTS

Tips for a Good Performance in Sight Reading

The sight reading test will be about 8 bars long and you'll have 30 seconds to look at the score. During that 30 seconds, you should look at the following things in the score and remember to play them correctly:

1. **Key signature**

2. **Accidentals**
   Accidentals (Sharps/ Flats/ Naturals) on the previous notes in the same bar.

3. **Easily mistaken notes:**
   D#, E#, A#, B#
   C^b, F^b, G^b
   Double sharps/ Double flats (e.g. D^x = E)

4. **Articulations**
   staccato/ legato (slurs)/ accents (>)

5. **Tempo markings and expressions (examples):**
Adagio	slow
Lento	slow
Andante	in a walking speed
Moderato	moderately
Allegretto	fairly quick
Allegro	quick
Con moto	with motion
Con brio	with spirit/ with vigour
Presto	very fast
Ritmico	rhythmically
Scherzando	playful
Giocoso	playful
Espressivo	expressive

6. **Dynamics (examples):**
f	loud
p	soft
cresc.	gradually getting louder
dim.	gradually getting softer

7. **Any difficult chords/ rhythms**

Giocoso

Andante

11

Andante

21

Andantino

22

31

Con brio

32

Moderato

Lively

33

Allegretto

34

Espressivo

Moderato

Notes

Printed in Great Britain
by Amazon